Fashion Illustration: Flat Drawing

p

Fashion Illustration: Flat Drawing

This is a Parragon Publishing book

Copyright © 2007 Parragon Books Ltd

Parragon Books Ltd
Queen Street House
4 Queen Street
Bath BA1 1HE, UK

Produced by Loft
Illustrations: Elena Sáez and Maite Lafuente
Text: Aitana Lleonart and Daniela Santos
Editorial coordinator: Catherine Collin
Art director: Mireia Casanovas Soley
Layout: Emma Termes Parera

US edition produced by Cambridge Publishing Management Ltd
Translator: Cynthia Stephens
Copy-editor: Sandra Stafford

ISBN: 978-1-4054-9432-8 (with jacket)
ISBN: 978-1-4075-0115-4 (without jacket)

Printed in China

Index

FLAT DRAWING

Within the world of fashion illustration there exists a discipline that is characterized by practical schematization and visualization of articles of clothing: flat drawing. Despite its apparent simplicity, to be able to capture all the details of the costumes one needs to be aware of certain aspects that are sometimes forgotten and that lend an article the distinctive characteristic that differentiates it from the rest.

The objective of this book is to provide the reference points and necessary variations for learning to draw plane designs for fashion in a simple and progressive manner. The advantage of this discipline is that it is not necessary to create human figures on which to illustrate the clothing, something that can become a complicated task depending on a person's skills. This book is directed at creative people who are not keen on drawing fashion models, and offers them the possibility of representing their ideas in a basic and functional manner without the necessity of applying them to the human body.

To start well it is necessary to remember a key concept of flat drawing for fashion: symmetry. The first step is to establish the axes of the structure: even though the garment includes asymmetric finishes, it is essential to represent each garment (shirts, coats, jackets, pants, or skirts) in a proportional manner starting from the central axis. This book provides, through its many examples, the tools necessary for achieving proportionality and coherence for all of the creations.

Although this branch of drawing may be visually less attractive, it is essential in the study and application of fashion design, in the introduction to pattern design, and in tailoring. It is not just concerned with showing current fashion trends, but rather with teaching appropriate techniques for putting into practice and giving expression to personal creativity in a clear and schematic manner.

This book offers many varieties and models of each type of garment: pants, blouses, jackets, shirts, underwear, and accessories. It also gathers together trends in costumes throughout the history of clothing. For example, in the section on pants the shapes and characteristics of each typology are illustrated, from the most formal and commonplace to the most diverse, for instance fishing pants, baggy pants, skirt pants, and pirate pants.

Everyone in the fashion world knows that what really confer a personal and distinctive aesthetic are accessories. For this reason, and because they play a fundamental role in the history of fashion throughout the centuries, a great variety of hats, shoes, belts, and purses are also included. These items are undoubtedly necessary for achieving a universal and stylistically complete creation.

Thanks to the numerous drawings that appear in these pages, the reader will be able to undertake research to stimulate their creativity and create multiple designs, as well as paying attention to all those details that normally pass unnoticed but that are extremely useful at the time of showing the shapes of the garments or the hang and personality of the materials—the tracing of the seams, the pleats or the creases.

This is a basic and practical book that feeds the imagination and helps to capture on paper every design in the closet.

Collars
Cuffs
Trimmings
Necklines

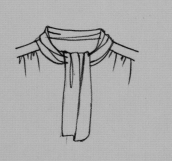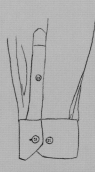

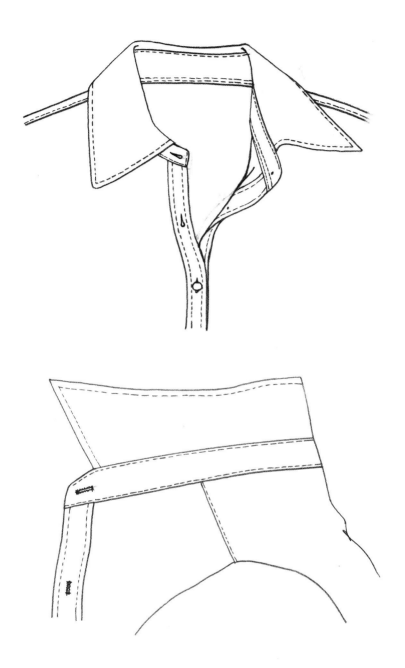

Shirt collar trims
Front and side view of a deep V-neck, with
backstitch and buttonhole trimmings

Collars

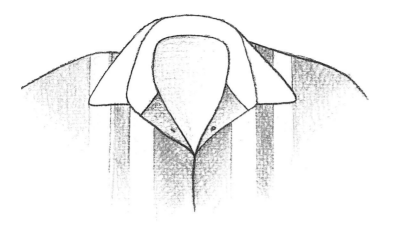

Polo shirt collar with button
This collar is somewhere between the formal and
the informal

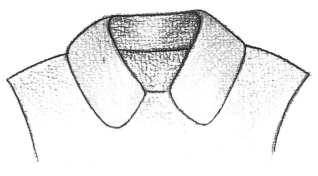

Double-sided baby collar
Also known as the Peter Pan collar, it is made from
two pieces of cloth that face each other and end in
round edges

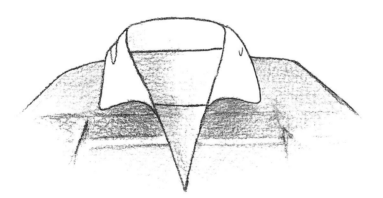

Polo neck collar open in a V
Variant of the traditional polo neck that substitutes
the buttons with a triangular piece of cloth

Tracksuit collar, sports garment
Round collar that closes with the same zipper
as the jacket

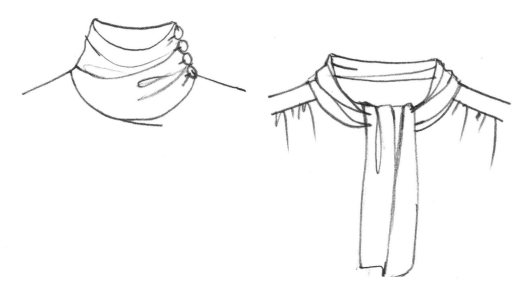

Buttoned turtle neck
Goes above the base of the neck and closes
with buttons behind or at the sides

Foulard
This collar incorporates a long, narrow
piece of cloth, gauze, or another light
material

Scarf
Represented as a long, wide piece of material
that encircles the neck

Bow
A longer foulard that ends in a
voluminous knot

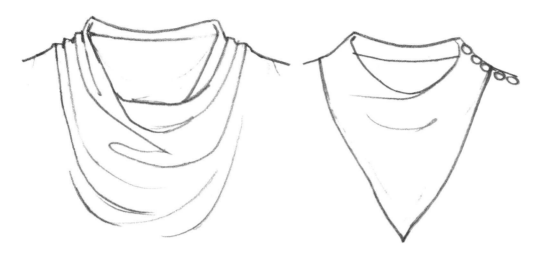

Draped neck
Neckline with a round or pointed cut that turns forward with a certain volume

Bandana
Of Hindu origin (*bandhana*, "to tie"), this triangle falls over the neckline toward the line of the bust

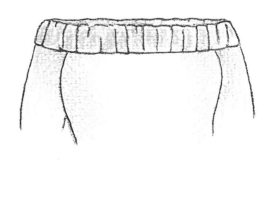

V-shaped collar with zipper
The most usual option for knitted sweaters

Elastic boat neck
Neckline hangs straight from shoulder to shoulder following the line of the collar bone

Plain lapel collar with button
Front part of the jacket, or coat, which is folded
and sewn to the collar

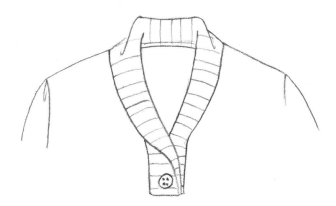

Lapel collar with button
The varieties of the style can be seen in trimmings
such as buttons or different textures

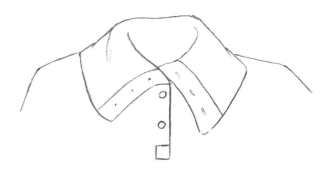

Double wrapover collar with button panel
Piece strengthened with double-width fabric or by
a material that is thicker than that of the jacket

Collar with an arabesque motif
Outlined by some elements of Arabic trims,
composed of geometric figures, leaf motifs, and
ribbons

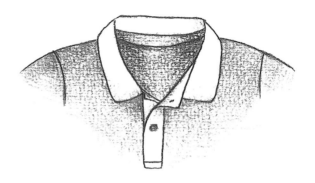

Polo neck collar with hook and eye
The characteristic polo neck collar and the feature
that distinguishes it from T-shirts

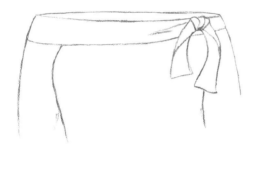

Large scoop collar with a bow
Leaves the shoulders bare and is finished off with a
figurative or genuine bow

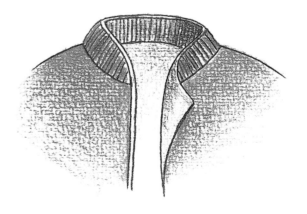

Sweater
Jacket of wool or another fabric, without a collar
and fastened at the front

Cuffs

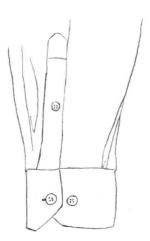

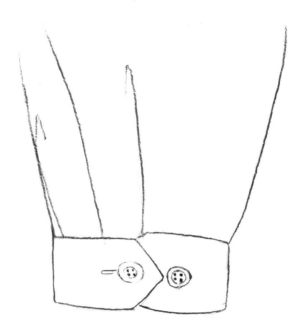

Pointed cuff
The most traditional and elegant, and the favorite
with formal wear such as a tuxedo

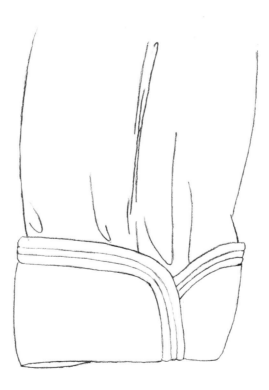

Turned-up cuff
Has its origin in the cuffs of masculine riding jackets
of the eighteenth century

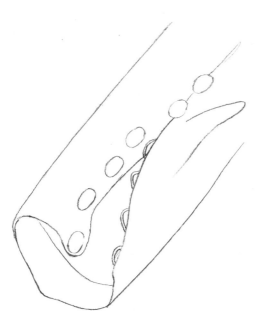

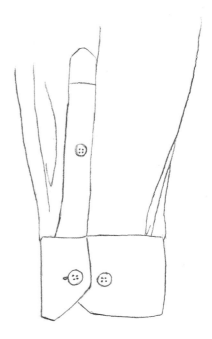

Cuff fastened with studs
One part of the cuff has been left open so that the fasteners can be seen

Cuff with cropped corners
One of the most popular sleeve endings for shirts

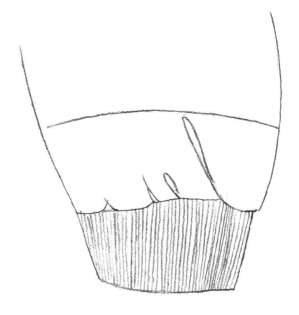

Elastic cuff
Characteristic of tracksuits, sweaters, and jackets

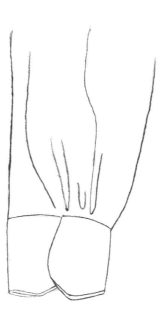

Shirt cuff in a wave form
Commonly used form for sleeve endings in blouses

Trimmings

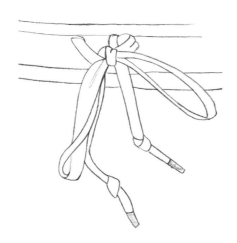

Shirt sleeve trim
The illustration focuses on the structural parts of the garment

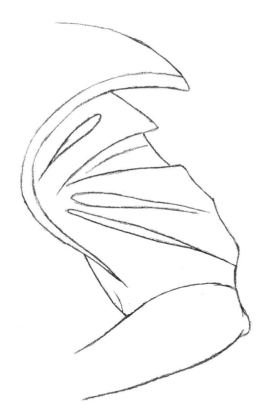

Half-sleeved shirt trim with bent elbow
Shows how the garment behaves with body movement

Full skirt pleats trim
Folds are sewn tightly over the hips: soft pleats give fullness to the skirt

Wide turned-up collar trim
Wider and higher than normal, this collar has a decorative purpose

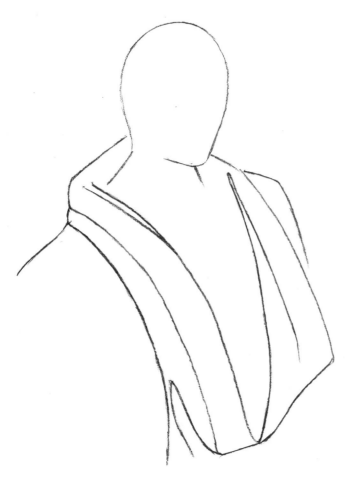

Long collar trim
Normally used in tight-fitting dresses and coats; was
very fashionable in the 1920s

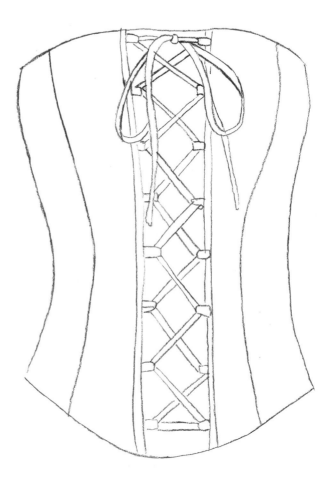

Lace-up trim for bodice
The lace-up regulates the pressure of the corset

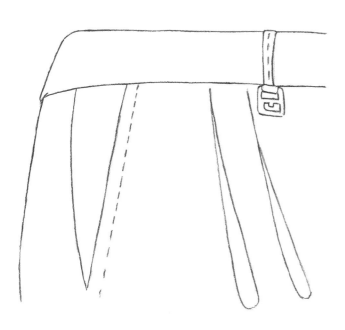

Pleats trim for pleated pants
The pleats below the waistband give fullness and freedom of movement

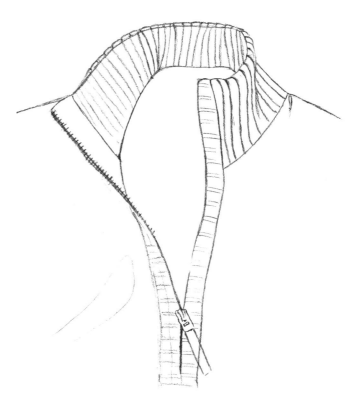

Collar with zipper
Shown half open to allow the tailoring trims from inside and outside to be seen

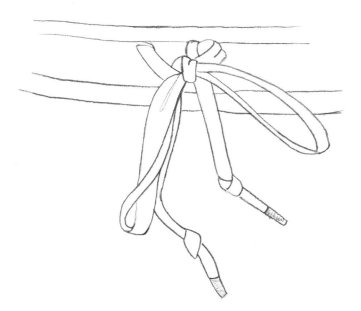

Knot trim
This detail is important when the knot forms part of the design of the garment or the accessory

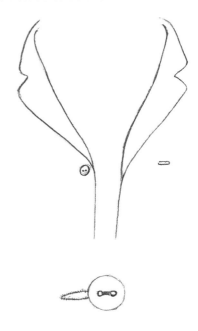

Button fastening trim on the collar of a jacket
The high seam included the buttons in feminine clothes from 1930 onward; prior to that they were used only in men's garments

Necklines

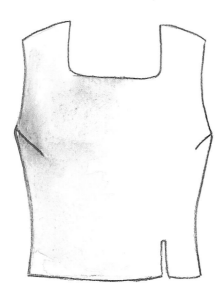

Square neck
Known also as a French neckline; frequently seen in feminine T-shirts

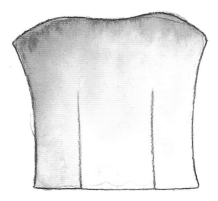

Sweetheart neckline
Follows the line of the bust, ending in a point at the heart; widely used in romantic dresses

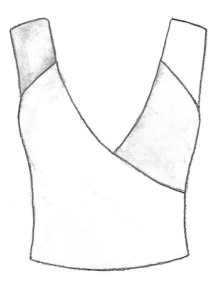

Imperial neckline
Falls toward the bust in the shape of a point or V; emphasizes generous busts and makes the shoulders stand out

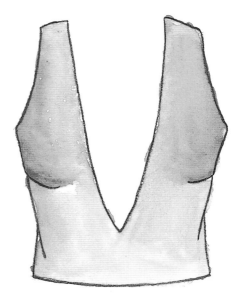

Long V-shaped neck
This neckline, which ends just above the waist, has been a favorite for designers in recent years

Collaret trim
Single gathered piece of cloth that falls over the shoulders and the bust; can also be used with a square neckline

Tear neckline
Falls in a rounded shape from the shoulders and ends in an wavy point at the level of the bust; its shape is like an inverted tear

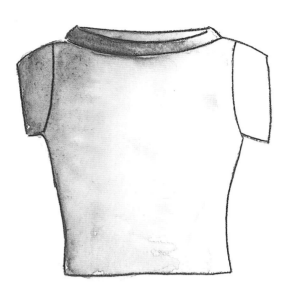

Boat neck
Forms a straight line that goes from the shoulders
or the collar bones; is elegant and discreet

Long collar
Neckline with a round or pointed cut, also known
as a draped neck because of the folds that provide
its volume

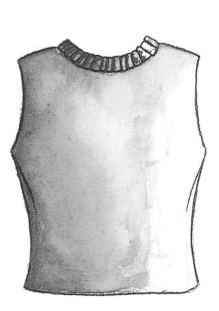

Cowl collar
Represented as a wider than normal neckline

Neckline with a collar gathered with cord
Widely used in peasant-style or romantic blouses

T-shirts
Shirts
Blouses
Sweaters

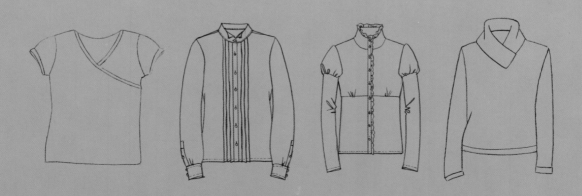

T-shirt
This versatile garment has become a staple of the
contemporary wardrobe

T-shirt with round collar
The most classic and widely used to give a sporty
look

Wrapover T-shirt with a V-neck
The inspiration for these T-shirts is the kimono

Shirts

Shirt with a yoke
The yoke is the upper part of the shirt or dress to which the neck, sleeves, and the rest of the garment are attached.

Straight shirt
Clean lines giving a basic style

Sleeveless shirt with a collar with pointed lapels
Its shape has evolved from the masculine vest

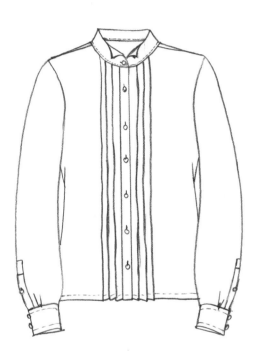

Dress shirt
White or very pale in color, this shirt must have a low collar for the bow tie and a double cuff for the cuff links

Shirt with mandarin collar
Heavily influenced by the popular Chinese style

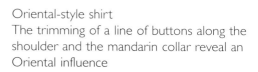

Oriental-style shirt
The trimming of a line of buttons along the shoulder and the mandarin collar reveal an Oriental influence

Denim shirt with a pocket
Has the pattern of a traditional shirt, but the pocket and the epaulets are essential for defining a casual air

Blouses

Gypsy
Blouse with a Bohemian inspiration that, because of
its structure, requires definition in its outline

Blouse with a knotted collar
Type of blouse that originates from a collar trim

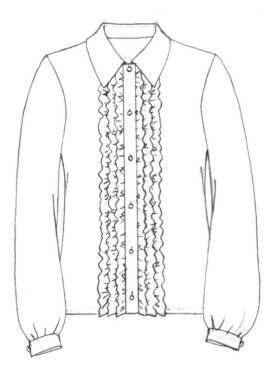

Peasant-style blouse
Associated with romantic styles, and for this reason
is drawn with diaphanous lines and gathers

Blouse with frills
Blouse with thin frontal strips that are sewn in
pleats and shaped like small flounces

Lace blouse with front panel
The lace combines easily with any kind of fabric and is often used in trimmings for both skirts and blouses

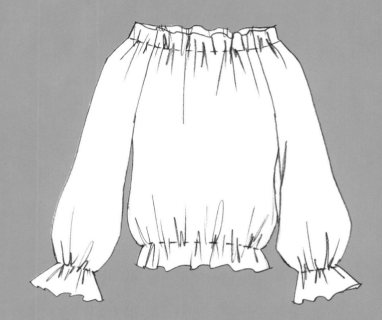

Blouse
Traditionally a peasant garment. In the twentieth century, this item transformed itself into a staple for all occasions and circumstances

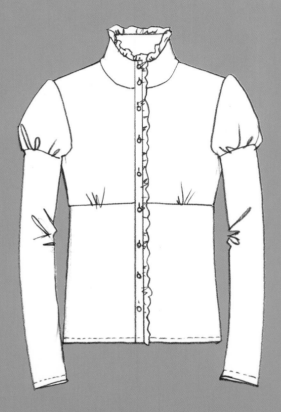

Victorian blouse
Direct descendant of the Victorian era, this garment
is fitted to the body, has small frills and gathers, and
a high collar

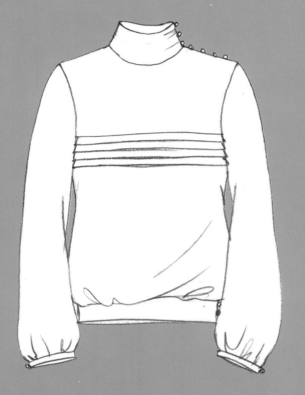

Blouse with buttons on the shoulder and pleats across
the chest
The row of folds are flat and act as an adornment;
they also shorten the length

Wide blouse with V-neck
Shown here with gathers at the cuffs and waist,
which give it volume

Caftan
Western version of the garment used by men and
women in the Near East; the length may fall at
various points between the hip and ankles

Sweaters

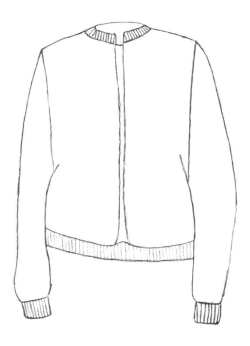

Sweater with a round collar
This sleeved and closed knitwear or cotton
garment can be identified by the elastic in the cuffs,
belt, and collar

Sweater with high wrapover collar
A staple garment with many different variations

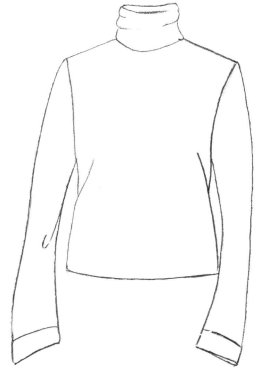

Sweater with a double collar and flared sleeves
The versatility of the collars and sleeves does not
alter the essence of the garment

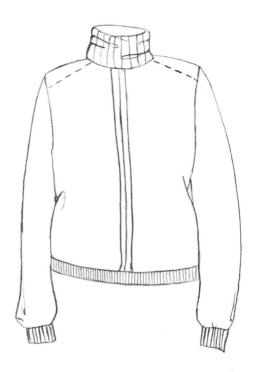

Sweater with a high collar, tight neckline, and sleeves
The rib is a style of knitting that is often used in high
collars because of its elastic effect

Sweater with a high loose-fitting and stylized collar, tight sleeves,
and elastic cuffs
This style should be worn with tight-fitting garments for best effect

Belted sweater
The opening at the front or at one side converts
the sweater into a jacket

Short top / Bolero
This version has the base structure of the
bolero jacket but is tailored in a finer material
that enables variants such as knots

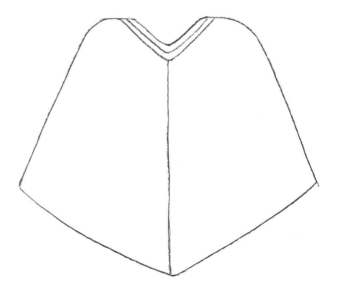

Vest with darts
This classic model ends in points, but unisex
interpretations throughout the 1980s have resulted in
rounded points and straight finishes

Mexican-style poncho
A warm garment with a simple cut that has been
adapted to *prêt-à-porter*

Jackets
Coats

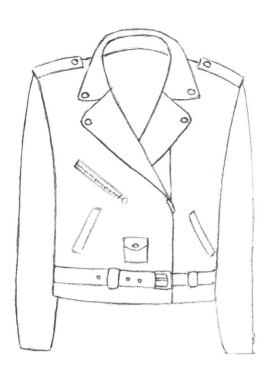

Leather jacket with zipper
From motorcyclists to rockers, this jacket defines a
certain style

Jacket with tailored lapels
A T-shirt with rounded collar worn underneath a
jacket with tailored lapels creates a contemporary
look

Jackets

Jacket with round double collar
This warm garment is shown short and adjusted to
the hip

Jacket with a tuxedo lapel
Masculine garment developed from the cut of a
riding coat; its unisex style means it is found in the
wardrobes of both men and women

Jacket with fitted lapel
At the end of the nineteenth century, when
women took up sports such as horse-riding or
tennis, this garment became part of their dress

Jacket with a chimney collar neckline
Since the eighteenth century, when it was born in
France as a garment for horse-riding, the jacket has
evolved like no other article of clothing

Neat sailor-style jacket
Double-breasted gold-button fastenings
characterize this classic from the high seas made of
blue woolen cloth

Short parka with hood
Waterproof jacket originally used by skiers, with
the addition of leather to the hood

Jacket with billfolds
The pockets become the protagonists thanks to
the billfold, the name given to the strip of cloth
that covers the opening

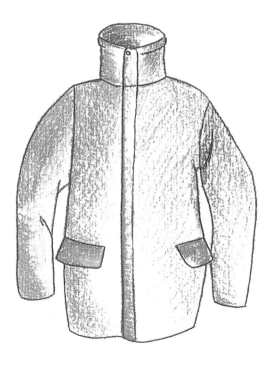

Denim jacket
Having seduced stars from the movies and rock-
and-roll during the 1950s, this jacket has long since
established itself as a staple of casual fashion

Double-collared three-quarter length parka
The puffed-out style suggests the quilted interior

Coats

Tailored coat with collar and lapel
The length of these coats does not allow for skirts
or dresses that are longer than them

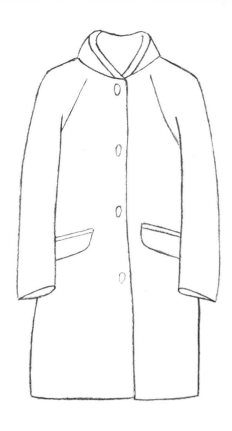

Coat with hood
This garment is a natural evolution from warm
cloaks

Straight coat open neck with lapel
Warm masculine garment that can be worn instead
of a suit jacket

Three-quarter length coat
A warm garment rather larger than a jacket

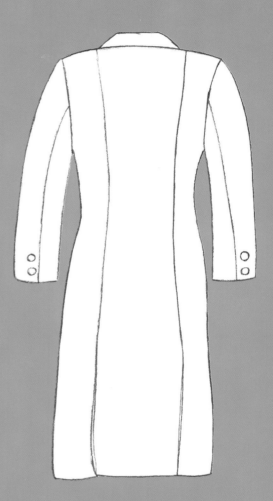

Long leather coat, front view
The seams at the sides and the collar create a lean, vertical look

Long leather coat, rear view
This diagram shows the position of trimmings on the back of the coat

Raincoat
The drawing shows the cape sewn on the shoulders, and the belt that characterizes this waterproof garment

Double-breasted raincoat with double button panel
Free version of a raincoat influenced by the design of warm coats

Pants

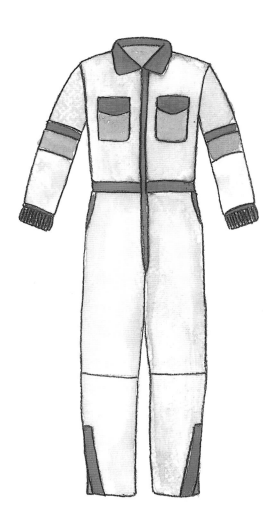

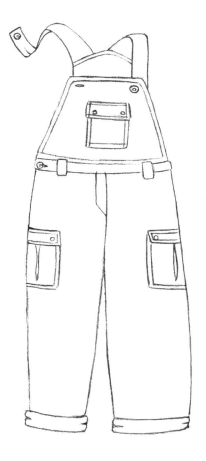

Quilted jumpsuit
Single-piece garment that can be represented with
variations in the pockets, fastening, and collar

Overalls
Maintains the characteristics of jeans, defined by
seams with backstitch, metallic buttons, and pockets

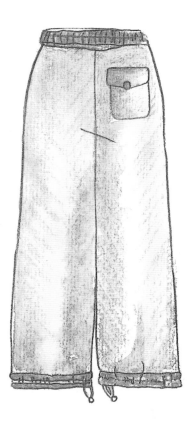

Wide fishing pants
Quite apart from the shape that defines them,
these pants must maintain their length just below
the knee

Tracksuit sports pants with cords on the legs
The characteristic of these pants is freedom of
movement and the ability to alter the width at the
bottom of the leg

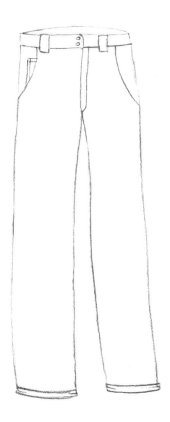

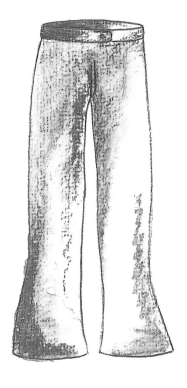

Straight pants
With typical masculine cut, straight vertical lines
predominate in these pants

Bell-bottoms
The pants widen as they reach the bottom of the
leg—a favorite in the disco era of the 1970s

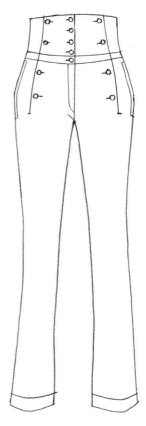

Cadet pants
Inspired by military uniforms of the eighteenth century, their fundamental characteristic is the lines of buttons on the sides

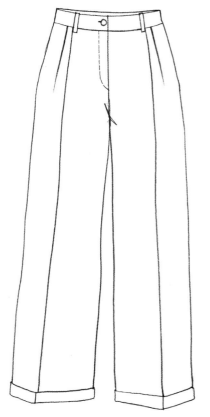

Baggy pants
Pants with very loose-fitting legs and accessorized with a belt fastened tightly in the high waistband—very popular in the 1990s

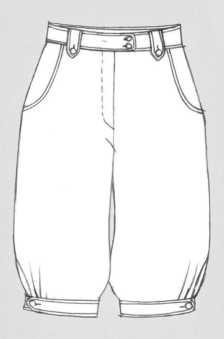

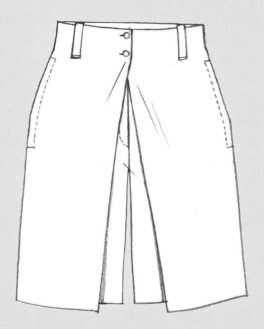

Hunting pants
Tight fitting at the knees, this model takes its
inspiration from the sport of hunting

Apron pants
Drawn here as two superimposed pieces of cloth,
the top one being like a skirt

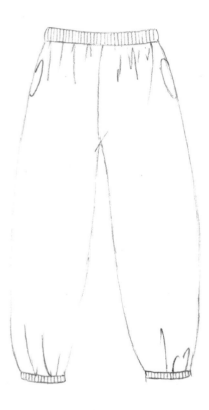

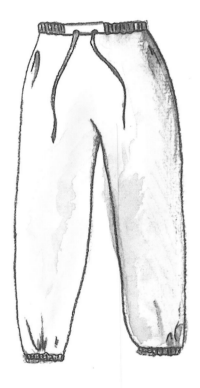

Tracksuit-style sports pants
Traditional representation of sports pants

Pajama pants
To distinguish them from the tracksuit a cord has
been added to the waist

Fashion Illustration: Plane Drawing

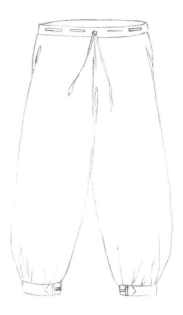

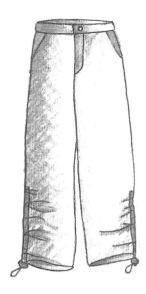

Loose-fitting pants
Garment with wide legs with gatherings at ankle level and pointed cuffs

Tracksuit-style sports pants with cords on the sides of the legs
This innovative trim means that this style is often used outside of the gym as a part of urban fashion

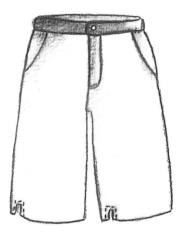

Short pants with trimmings at the bottom
This garment is not now exclusively used on the beach or for playing sport; those with pure lines and restrained colors form part of a city closet

Short skirt pants
Wide open skirt that is sewn down the center like pants

Short safari pants
Bermudas that are represented with characteristic
backstitches, generally in khaki or military green

Balloon pants with bow
Feminine garment similar to short baggy pants

Sarvel pants
To show the special cut of these pants, they are represented open and extended

Samurai pants
This garment, which takes its shape from ancient Japanese military pants, is crossed in front and knotted at the waist over a sash

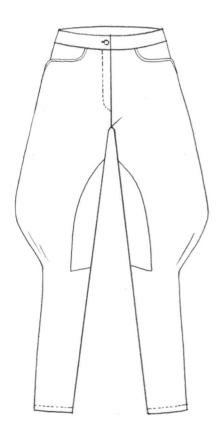

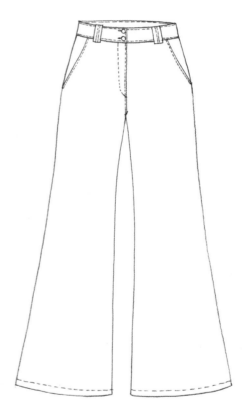

Jodhpurs
Very baggy down to the knee and then they get thinner, tightening toward the ankle; they are used for horse-riding

Flared pants
The legs starts to widen at the level of the pockets and reach their maximum volume at the wearer's feet

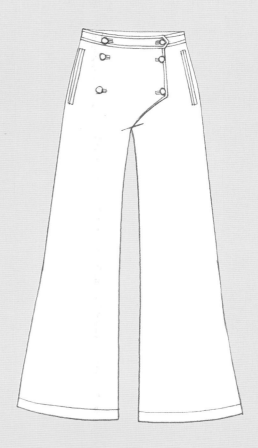

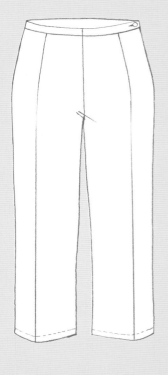

Sailor pants
Typically with a frontal piece that is fastened along the side in lines of three buttons, and with very wide leg bottoms

Pirate pants
Also known as Capri pants, they reach the knees, or a little below, and adjust themselves to the figure

Skirts
Dresses

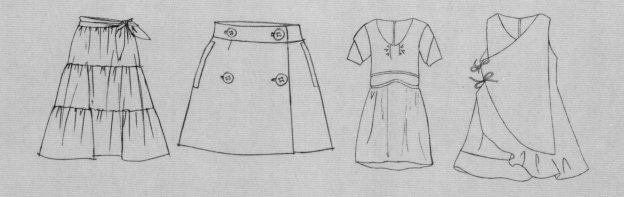

Full skirt
The spread is represented by the triangular shape
and the impression of volume

Denim-style skirt, rear view
The perspective from the back of this skirt shows
the similarity of its cut to that of jeans

Skirts

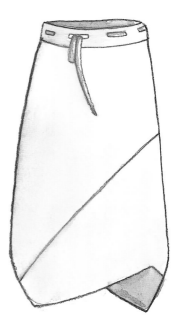

Plain asymmetric skirt
Modern variation of a traditional skirt

Full asymmetric skirt
The effect of movement is key in the
representation of this garment

Short plain skirt
With a straight cut, it reaches just above the knees;
consequently it is slightly longer than a mini-skirt

Trapezoidal shaped skirt with ribbon
Garment that is fashionable as a beach wrap and is
tied at the waist

Skirt with satin flounces
The flounces give volume and movement

Skirt with gathered flounces
This shorter variant shows a greater volume thanks
to the gathers in the flounces

Skirt with cuts and spread
A cut that widens toward the hem gives this style
its amplitude

Peasant-style skirt
Traditionally gathered and reaching the ankles

Denim skirt with round pockets
The reinterpretation of the traditional denim skirt
is achieved with minor modifications such as the
shape of the pockets

Denim skirt with flounces
A way of achieving a lighter volume

Petticoat skirt
Represented as a wide skirt, generally white and incorporating lace

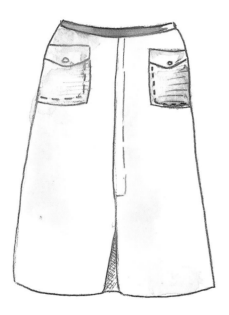

Long denim skirt
With their minimal or non-existent spread, the straight lines in this style predominate

Pleated skirt
From Coco Chanel to Wimbledon, pleated skirts
have always been at the front of fashion

A-line skirt
André Courrèges and Pierre Cardin set this shape
in the 1960s

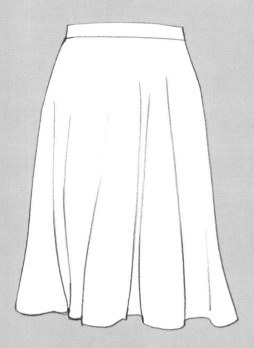

Bias skirt
Arose from a technique of the 1930s whereby the cloth was cut on the bias, allowing the material to fall in an attractive and flattering way

Cancan skirt with tutu
Takes its shape from the skirts of the famous dancers who performed in the dance halls of Montparnasse, Paris

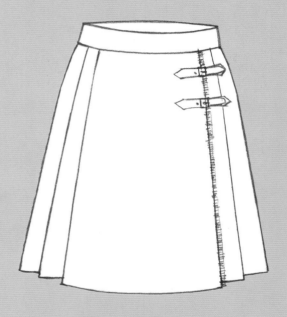

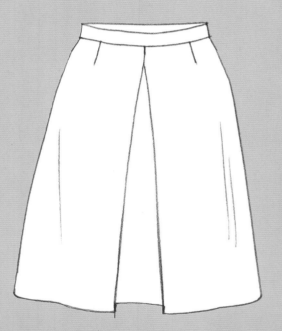

Plaid skirt
This garment should be shown pleated and with an
opening at the side, just as the Scots conceived it
for riding on horseback

Gusset skirt
The front gusset appears like a large panel that
gives it movement

Ball-shaped skirt
This garment, which fascinated Cristóbal Balenciaga, is tightened at the hem by means of a piece of elastic that is invisible but creates the inflated shape

Safari skirt
Shown here with a high waist and characteristic back-stitches, generally in a khaki or military green color

Dresses

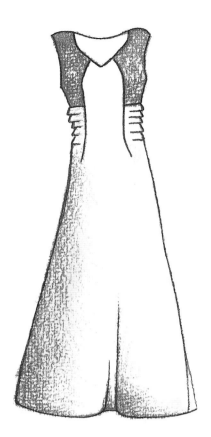

Dress with tucks
Dresses are ideal for ornamental options like
this, which comprise a variety of hem lengths

Halter-neck dress
Shown with an accentuated cut for the
armhole at armpit level, often called an
American armhole

Dress gathered at the chest and waist
Garment with straight lines, very popular in the
1920s

Dress with a wrapover flounce
Inspired from old-fashioned underwear garments

Underwear
Accessories

Japanese wrapover bathrobe
Represented as a loose-fitting and comfortable
garment that brings to mind Japanese kimonos

Shirt-like bathrobe with yoke
Alternatives can be created with aesthetic options
such as a yoke or a tailored waist

Woman's bathrobe
Acquires a feminine profile because of the
trimmings and color

Man's bathrobe
The wide sleeves and large pockets give it a
masculine character

Underwear

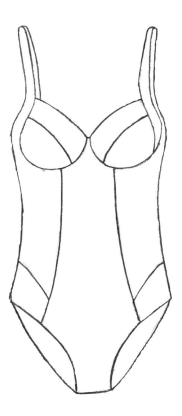

"Balconet" leotard
This garment has been designed to show off the figure, hence the seams around the hips, abdomen, and bust

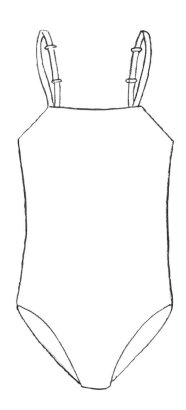

Sports leotard
Distinguished from the "Balconet" by its simpler neckline and absence of seams

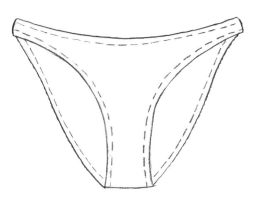

Brazilian panties
They cover slightly more than the tanga and less than conventional panties

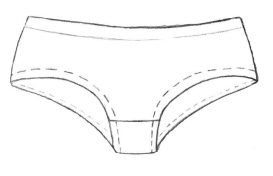

Panties with a low waist
Pin-up inspiration for this garment that has a similar structure to old-fashioned French knickers

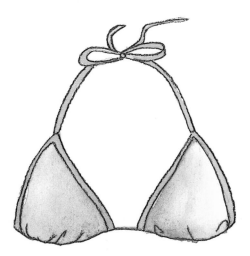

Triangular bikini bra with tie at neck
Fastened at the back of the neck with a knot or a
brooch

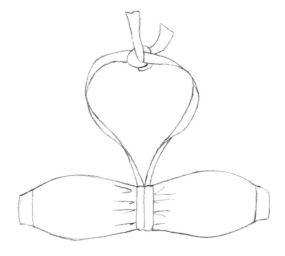

Sash-type bikini bra
Can be fastened just at the back and / or with a
knot behind the neck

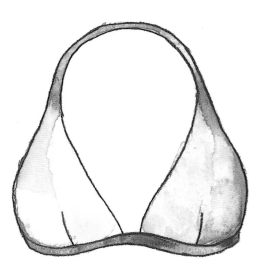

Triangular bikini bra
Its basic geometric composition has converted it
into a classic; the variants show themselves in the
ways in which it is fastened

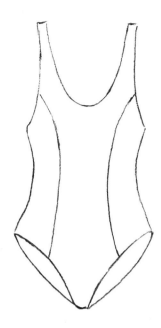

Swimsuit with darts
Goes from the groin to the chest and
normally leaves most of the back uncovered

Shapely swimsuit
Most widely used for swimming as a sport; the
curved seams give a flattering shape to the figure
and facilitate movement

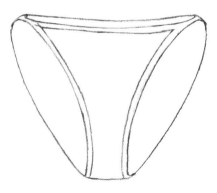

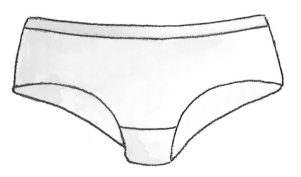

Pantie bikini
The thin strips on the sides distinguish it from the
Brazilian pantie

Shorty low waist
Has the same structure as the low-waist pantie,
but the illustration gives it color to distinguish it as
a bathing suit

Accessories

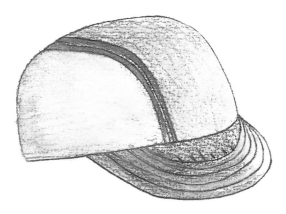

Cap with military-style visor
The curved shapes of the crown and the peak, as well as the color, give it a military character

Unisex sports cap
Its fundamental characteristic is an enormous peak

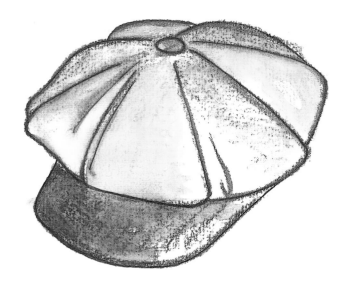

Wide cap
A direct descendant of the beret, it maintains its basic construction with segments of cloth

Half-brimmed hat
The brim is rolled up at the back, represented in a turn-up

Tweed hat
The drawing reveals the network of fabric threads, and suggests that it refers to a hat with a rigid structure

Sailor's hat
The curve-shaped crown characterizes this hat inspired by sailors' uniforms

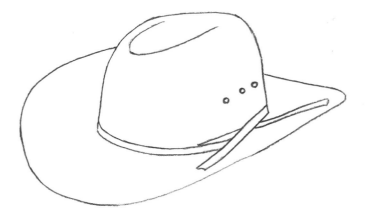

Denim cowboy hat
Example that the cowboys adapted from the Mexican hat; it is identified by the wide brim which is lightly folded at the edges

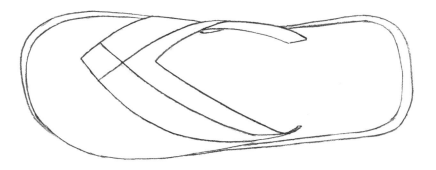

Flip-flop sandal
View from above the shoe, which consists of
just two pieces: the insole and the straps
that hook around the toes

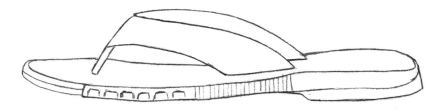

Profile of flip-flop sandal
This allows the details of the design to be seen—
for example, the low heel and wide straps

Military-style boot
Also known as "Dr. Martens" because of the name
of their inventor; they were an icon of the punk
aesthetic

Country boot
Synonymous with Texan or cowboy boots, they are
characterized by lateral elevations that make it
easier to put them on, and by the high heel

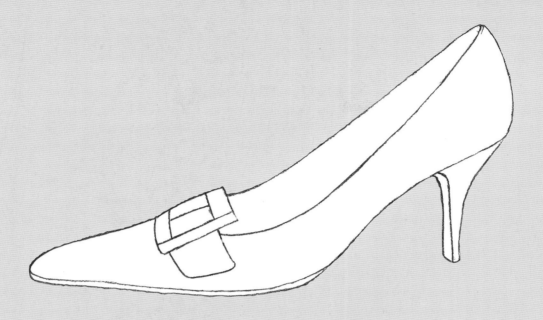

High-heeled shoes
The variety of designs generate real works of art;
one of the best creators is the shoemaker Manolo
Blahnik

Elegant high-heeled shoes with a strap around the heel
Simple lines and a lack of ornamentation to illustrate a staple

Moccasin
Shoe without cords or buckles, made from just one
piece of untanned leather in imitation of the
handcrafted footwear that is characteristic of North
American Indians

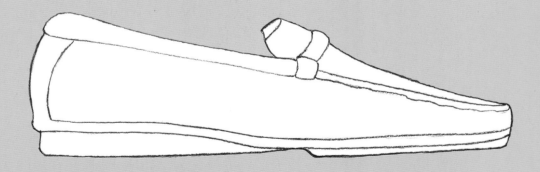

Profile of moccasin
The close-up shows the absence of a heel, typical
of this type of shoe

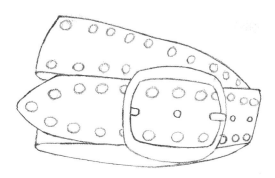

Belt with metallic studs
Used as an accessory for a casual look, preferably
with denim pants or skirts

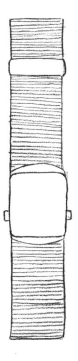

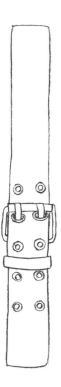

Military-style belt
Made from a resistant fabric, without holes due to
the pressure buckle

Plain belt
Narrows the waist in skirts, pants, and dresses

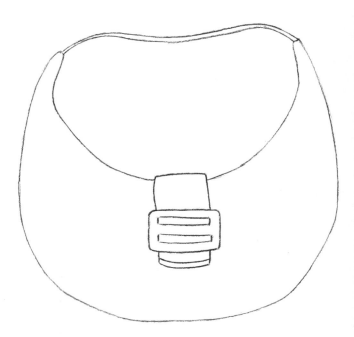

Trapezoidal-shaped purse
Has very short handles that merge with the body
of the bag

Purse in the shape of a half moon
Large-sized buckles are a constant for fashionable
bags

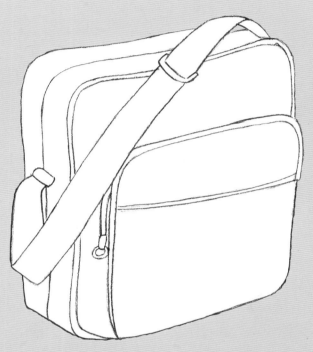

Tweed purse
The retro air is emphasized by returning to the
traditional shape of a change purse

Sling bag
Also known as a shoulder bag; it crosses over the
chest and leaves the hands free

Index